WELCOME TO TOKYO

Located 35°41'N 139°41'E, TOKYO is the biggest city in Japan. Even people living in TOKYO don't know everything about it. TOKYO is quickly becoming like other capital hubs. International brands can be found everywhere. This book will only show you the authentic face of TOKYO. Japan is a Far East country that has given rise to an interesting culture and unique items. You should feel and enjoy the original TOKYO. Your memories of sightseeing can degrade over time, but souvenirs will maintain your memories forever; so shop more.

CONTENTS

¥5 & ¥50

"Try to find some coins from your birth year! Don't forget to convert to the Japanese year."

Have you already exchanged your money to yen? Do you have any of these coins? These Japanese coins have holes in them. They are unique, right? Some people wear them as charms. In Japan, ¥5 coins are considered very lucky; the Japanese for "5 yen", means luck. You should keep a few when you go back home.

GATSBY

Japan is a country that prides itself on cleanliness. You can find cleaning products everywhere. These body sheets come in a wide array of scents and serve a variety of purposes. Disinfecting, drying, deodorizing and different degrees of cooling are just a few of the types available. It is remarkable how many different ones there are! They are easy to use and perfect for traveling.

Starting at ¥378

Available at most drugstores and convenience stores.

PARK HYATT TOKYO

One of Tokyo's most prestigious hotels, Park Hyatt Tokyo is a very conceptual hotel. The Gutsy sculpture above the front entrance was created by artist Mieko Yuki, and welcomes you during your stay. A hand sized Gutsy figure is available for sale at Delicatessen. If you put this in your home's entrance you can experience a similar atmosphere to Park Hyatt Tokyo. Gutsy ornament ¥33000

 3-7-1-2 Nishi-Shinjuku Shinjuku-Ku Tokyo ☎03-5322-1234 www.tokyo.park.hyatt.com

The 52nd floor of Park Hyatt Tokyo features the New York Grill. Showcasing an amazing view of the city, it also has an open kitchen where you can watch the chefs prepare your food.

New York Grill ☎03-5323-3458

Delicatessen, is on the first floor. Sandwiches, cakes and many other food items are available for sale. You can also pick up a special black apron or oven mitt with a simple yet cool design.

Apron ¥6000 Mitten ¥2400

DELICATESSEN ☎03-5323-3635

ISETAN

Isetan is one of the most famous department stores in Japan. The Shinjuku headquarters location features many well known brands. The company's trademark is an original tartan plaid pattern which is featured on the store's shopping bags. There are two pattern types, one for the men's store and one for the main store. If you buy something at Isetan you will receive this bag for free, otherwise it can be purchased from a machine at the store's entrance. free with purchase. on its own: paper bag ¥100 vinyl bag ¥1000

3-14-1 Shinjuku Shinjuku-Ku Tokyo ☎03-3352-1111

TOKYU-HANDS

Tokyu-hands is a special creative life store that carries thousands of useful items. It is a definite must-stop shop for tourists. Tokyu-hands carries the brand TORAY which is a "super fabric" manufacturer. These undershirts are available for both men and women. They come in a variety of colors and are specially designed for travel. They are comfortable and immediately dry when they are washed. This is one of Japan's futuristic items. starting at ¥1728

2F-8F 5-24-2 Sendagaya Shibuya-ku Tokyo ☎03-5361-3111
shinjuku.tokyu-hands.co.jp (16 branches in Tokyo)

This torso charm is an iconic item of the school. It is modelled after a real torso on a 1:19.4 scale. ¥411

BUNKA FASHON COLLEGE

Many Japanese designers have graduated from this specialized fashion college. This make-up kit is a collaboration with the famous cosmetics company Shiseido. The kit includes everything you need to do your make-up, and is available in one compact set. The colors change yearly to match the latest trends. If you are looking for some new make-up you should check out this school's gift shop. ¥30858

3-22-1 Yoyogi Shibuya-Ku Tokyo ☎03-3299-2029 www.bunka-fc.ac.com

Fashion students often use these weights to hold down papers or fabrics while they work on their designs. It is difficult to find this ideal type of weight. Even thought they are a bit heavy, you should bring a few back. silver ¥659 colors ¥767

KINOKUNIYA

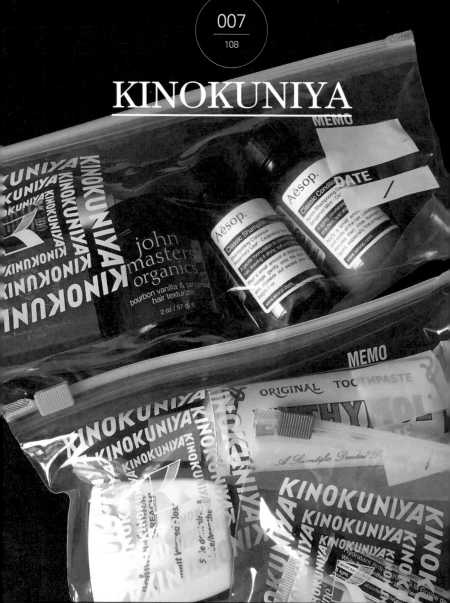

Kinokuniya is an upscale supermarket. Established in Aoyama in 1910, it was the first store in Japan to use shopping carts. The store carries many original items, including this simple bag with a practical slide tab. It is useful and has a stylish design. ¥164 (S /16 bags M / 14 bags L /10 bags)

Ao Building B1F 3-11-7 Kita-Aoyama Minato-Ku TOKYO
☎03-3409-1231 www.e-kinokuniya.com (14 branches in Tokyo)

CHRISTOPHER NEMETH

Christopher Nemeth was a UK designer from Birmingham. He moved to Tokyo in 1986 and designed unique cutting patterns for clothes. Nemeth's legendary brand recently partnered with Louis Vuitton making it even more renowned. True to his style, these button pins add an interesting touch to anything you pin them to.

¥300 - 1000 each

HEAD PORTER TOKYO

The world renowned brand, Porter, makes a special material called "Tanker".
It was inspired by bomber jackets and is famous in Japan. Only Head Porter
carries navy blue Tanker bags. It is a rare and beautiful, shiny navy color.
Lightweight and heavy duty, it is perfect for all your travels.

Left/ 2WAY WAIST BAG ¥13716   Right/ 2 WAY BOSTON BAG ¥27540

 3-21-12 Jingumae Shibuya-Ku Tokyo ☎03-5771-2621 www.headporter.co.jp

GOOD DESIGN SHOP
COMME des GARÇONS D&DEPARTMENT PROJECT

D and Department takes old items and upcycles them into creative pieces. They also carry a wide selection of interesting storage items. These boxes are available in different colors depending on the season. Use them to store your items in a trendy and organized way. Starting at ¥1026

GYRE 2F 5-10-1 Jingumae Shibuya-Ku Tokyo ☎03-3406-2323

Y.S. PARK

There are many hair salons in Japan, and many stylists use this comb. The holes on the side are spaced 1 cm apart so it is easy to recognize how much hair is being cut. The comb is also heat and chemical resistant and fits nicely in your hand. Available in many colors and sizes this is a great and very useful product. ¥1080. prices vary depending on size.

Y.S.PARK Omote-sando 4-29-3 jingumae shibuya-ku, Tokyo ☎03-3746-2244

TOKYU DEPARTMENTSTORE
TOYOKO STORE

Near Shibuya scramble, there is a famous Hachiko statue. On the second floor of the adjacent Tokyu department store there is a souvenir shop with many Hachiko inspired items. This is a traditional masu cup used for special occasions. Enjoy the natural white cedar feel and aroma as you drink your favorite sake. ¥864 each

2-24-1 Shibuya-Ku Shibuya ☎03-3477-3111 www.tokyu-dept.co.jp

DRESSTERIOR

A&S

DRESSTERIOR is a select boutique in Japan. Its main shop is in Shibuya. The building's interior and exterior bear an original atmosphere. Kazuyasu Mori is the creative director of the brand and he is in charge of everything. His ideas are very smart. This agenda includes a built-in wallet and credit card slots. It is a must have all-in-one item.   ¥31320

JINNAN HONTEN 1-6-5 Jinnan Shibuya-ku Tokyo ☎03-5457-2431(6 branches in Tokyo)

YUJI

Yuji is a master of beef. His Tokyo shop always serves fresh meat and everyday there are long lines to get in. Yuji collaborated with Kama-asa shoten, a shop in Kappa bashi with a century long history, to create the perfect original roaster. Each roaster comes with two interchangeable racks depending on your grilling needs, and has a special serial number on the main unit. If you provide this serial number to Yuji you can buy beef directly from him.   ¥19800

11-1 Udagawacho Shibuya-Ku TOKYO ☎03-3464-6448 http://yakiniku-yuji.com

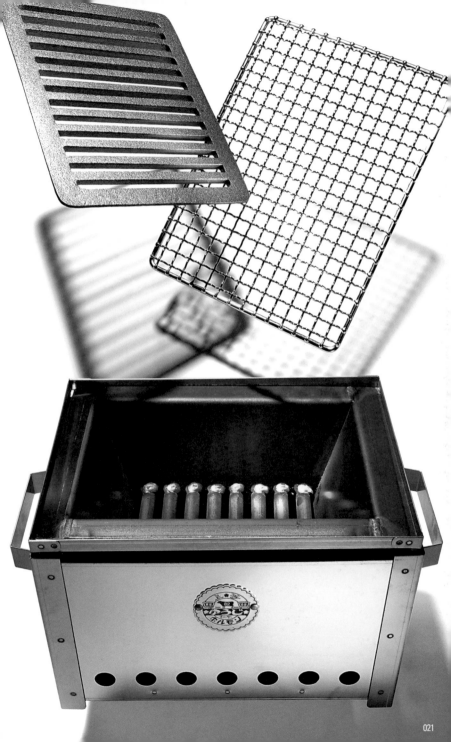

DELFONICS

Delefonics imports a lot of foreign stationary, offering fresh items to Japanese customers. At the same time, the store creates its own original items. These document cases are a best seller. Available in a variety of colours, the vinyl cases are easy to care for, lightweight and practical.

starting at ¥220

B1 PARCO PART1 15-1 Udagawacho Shibuya-Ku TOKYO
☎03-3477-5949 www.delfonics.com (14 branches in Tokyo)

KUUMBA

KUUMBA BOOKSHOP
a division of traveling book nook ®

016
108

Kuumba is known for its incense. They have over 350 different scents, so it is possible to use a different one every day of the year. "Sweetrain" is the brand's best seller. If you like incense you should take the time to choose your favorite. Kuumba also carries this unique incense holder. The incense hangs upside down in a canister amplifying the aroma.

Jumbo ¥10880 Regular ¥9800

KUUMBA BOOKSHOP 2-45-6 Tomigaya Shibuya-Ku Tokyo
☎03-5452-1698 kuumbainternational.com

OKURA

OKURA Japan has a special history with the color indigo. Japanese denim for example, is considered to be the best quality in the world. Okura stocks many indigo items. The shop has an everlasting old Japanese atmosphere. Okura's indigo is beautiful and becomes even more stunning with time. Although they have lots of items you should try the indigo sweatshirts. Many people wear indigo colored bottoms, but you should give an indigo colored top a try.

¥18360

20-11 Sarugakucho Shibuya-Ku Tokyo ☎03-3461-8511 www.hrm.co.jp/okura

「またたびボール」

またたびボールは、猫の大好きなおもちゃです。
またたびの木で編まれた外籠の中にはその剥いだ樹皮が
ぎゅっと詰められている、「またたび」のみで作られた
工芸品です。

BENIYA MINGEITEN

This shop carries many traditional Japanese items. In Japan cats are known
to love silvervine. If you have a cat, or know someone who has a cat, this
100% silvervine ball will make a purr-fect present.   ¥486 each

2-7-1 Minami aoyama Minato-Ku Tokyo ☎03-5875-3261 beniya.m78.com

MAGNIFLEX

Mesh wing

Magniflex is the biggest sleeping product company in Florence, Italy. It is famous in Japan too. This company does not use any springs, making it good for your body and the environment. This model is available only in Japan, and is perfect for the typical Japanese life style. In fact it is one of Magniflex's best sellers. It is easy to carry and can fold up to fit into Tokyo's compact apartments. The quality is really high and inspires good bodily health. If you are interested in this product don't miss it during your Japanese travels. Starting at ¥33858(single)

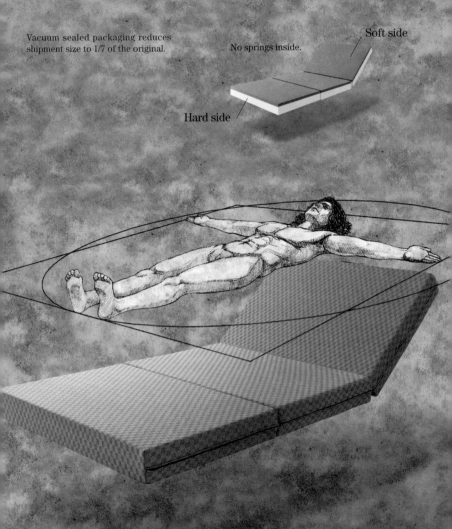

Vacuum sealed packaging reduces shipment size to 1/7 of the original.

No springs inside.

Soft side

Hard side

Mesh wing Leonardo

The Leonardo Mesh Wing is the deluxe version of the original mesh wing. It is made of two layers creating a more comfortable feel. You can recognize it by its distinctive check pattern. The company has so much confidence in the product that they named it after Italy's most famous polymath, Leonardo da Vinci. Starting at ¥49950(single)

Omotesando showroom 2F 3-5-5 Kita-aoyama Minatto-Ku Tokyo
☎ 0120-008-604

JINGU STADIUM

The Tokyo Yakult Swallows are the city's professional baseball team. Their home stadium is in the centre of Tokyo. When the team gets a point, Swallows fans use a mini umbrella as a sign of their support. They also have a unique cheer and sing a traditional Tokyo festival song. If you have the chance to watch a baseball game in Tokyo you should get this umbrella. Go Swallows!

3-1 Kasumigaokachou Shinjuku-Ku Tokyo
☎03-3404-8999 http://www.jingu-stadium.com/

gingam JAPAN

The Austrian brand Swarovski is famous for providing luxury crystals all over the world. gingam JAPAN is one of the best technical factories in the world, that can apply Swarowski crystals with a special technique to many different items. This belt is very difficult to make because the shape is always bending, but it rarely looses any crystals. The belt is bright and the workmanship is precise. This piece will add sparkle to your style.

¥86400(many colors available)

World Styling Corporaltion
2-18-21 Jingumae Shibuya-Ku Tokyo ☎03-6804-1554 www.wwwsssccc.jp/

KOMACHI BENI

If you only try one lipstick in Japan you should try this one. Since ancient times, Japanese women have been using beni or Benibana (safflower) to adorn their lips. Painted onto a cup, this lip colour is green until you add water to it, at which point it turns red. Depending on the amount you apply, you can customize your shade from a pink hue to a deep scarlet. ¥19440

ISEHAN HONTEN 6-6-20 MinamiAoyama Minato-Ku Tokyo ☎03-5774-0296
www.isehanhonten.co.jp

THE CONTEMPORARY FIX

This shop has a delicatessen on the first floor which serves a weekly-changing seasonal menu. The second floor features a trendy boutique. MR.GENTLEMAN is one of the brands they carry. It often features the slogan "AOYAMA　CITY" which can be found on many items throughout the shop. Aoyama is the most fashionable area in Tokyo, and this shop will show you Tokyo's latest trends.

 3-12-14 Kita-aoyama Minato-Ku Tokyo 2F THE CONTEMPORARY FIX
☎03-6418-1460 www.thecontemporaryfix.com

TOTAL Workout

TOTAL Workout is a famous training gym in Japan. All of their equipment and training machines have a special red design. Working with Porter, TOTAL Workout created a special gym bag with its signature red detail. The bag is lightweight and has a special compartment for shoes. It also includes an additional roll up bag that can be used to store sweaty gym clothes.

¥52,500

B2F 6-4-1 Roppongi Minato-Ku Tokyo ☎03-5414-1102
www.totalworkout.jp (additional location in Shibuya)

HOTEL OKURA TOKYO

A timeless hotel in the city, Hotel Okura Tokyo has many fans all over the world. This hotel is a real classic. Available in the hotel's gift shop, these original mints have a refreshing, yet mild taste. The tin looks elegant and cool, and it can be refilled with your favorite mints. ¥540

2-10-4 Toranomon Minato-Ku Tokyo ☎03-3582-0111 www.hotelokura.co.jp/tokyo

SHIBA DAIJINGU

A big shrine in Tokyo, Shiba Daijingu carries a charm popular with the ladies. This charm brings good luck and more clothes. If you like fashion you should get this charm. It is said to promote a happy life for women, but if you are a fashionable man, you can buy this too. Chigibako ¥800- ¥1200

1-12-7 Shibadaimon Minato-Ku Tokyo ☎03-3431-4802 www.shibadaijingu.com

HIMIKO&HOTALUNA

027

108

Tokyo is a water city and many ships can be seen sailing around its harbor. You should book a pass for the Himiko or Hotaluna if you are in the area. These ships were designed by Reiji Matsumoto, a renowned creator of futuristic cartoons. They are beautiful, sleek and look like space ships from the future. Model kit ¥2500 ChoroQ ¥900

1/150 Scale
未来型水上バス

ヒコ

未来型水上バス
ヒコ

Departing from Asakusa, Hinode Pier and Odaiba Seaside Park
www.suijobus.co.jp/ship/himiko.html ☎ 0120-977-311

RED FEATHER

October 1st is a day of charitable donation in Japan. In front of most train stations there are people standing with boxes and feathers. If you donate money you will get a red feather with some adhesive tape on the back, that can be worn to show your support. Donations go to a charity community that aids a variety of causes. pay what you can

TOKYO TOWER

One of the city's most prominent landmarks,
Tokyo Tower is a 333 meter broadcasting tower.
It was opened in 1958 and has two observation decks.

Let's post a
letter with an
original postmark
from
Tokyo Tower !

xoxo

Naoki Kokubo
World Photo Press
3-39-2 Nakano,
Nakano - Ku
Tokyo 164-8551
JAPAN

Tokyo tower has many cool products and lots of things to see. One unique thing
you can do is send a specially marked letter or postcard when you mail it from
the tower's first observation deck. This postmark is unique to Tokyo tower.

 4-2-8 Shiba-kouen Minato-Ku Tokyo ☎03-3433-5111 www.tokyotower.co.jp

高得点
こうとくてん

On the highest floor, by special request, you can obtain this good luck charm. It will bring you high scores on your tests, or in games. ¥250

UKA NAIL OIL

From a famous hair salon, Uka nail oil is uniquely named after a specific time. The times represent different scents and properties. This oil is good for your nails and for your mind. The rollerball makes application easy and the scented oil provides moisture for your cuticles encouraging healthy nail growth. Starting at ¥3240

UKA ROPPONGI MIDTOWN 9-7-4 Akasaka Minato-Ku Tokyo ☎03-5413-7236
www.uka.co.jp (6 branches in Tokyo)

STARBUCKS COFFEE

Available only at the Meguro headquarters location, these mugs are made in select workshops and out of special materials. The White mug- made with a particular warm white varnish, this mug creates a bold contrast with your coffee. The Black mug- the pigmentation is like charcoal and appears to change colors bringing zen into your life. It carries with it a special atmosphere. Enjoy the mugs on their own, or as a complimentary pair.

White Latte Mug (320mℓ) ¥1520・(390mℓ) ¥1720   Charcoal Mug (380mℓ) ¥2670・(400mℓ) ¥2670

SUNSHINE AQUARIUM

032

108

Located on the top floor of a building, this famed aquarium is home to many types of aquatic creatures. Sunshine Aquarium has a strong city vibe. They have lots of good souvenirs including these cute otter and penguin castanets. Fun to play, you should give these a try.   ¥496 each

Daiogusokumushi is a giant isopod and the inspiration behind these slippers.
Envisioned by a handler at the aquarium, this is a very unusual looking
slipper. When you wear these sensational slippers, everyone will be curious
about them. ¥2592

World import mart Top Floor Sunshine City 3-1 Higashi Ikebukuro Toshima-Ku
☎03-3989-3466 www.sunshinecity.co.jp/aquarium

JIYU GAKUEN MYONICHIKAN

Jiyu Gakuen Myonichikan used to be a women's school. The building was designed by the famous architect Frank Lloyd Wright and his team. His design is very symmetrical and beautiful. The building is now used for special events like weddings, concerts and important lectures. The building also houses a gift shop that carries special cork building blocks. You can use your imagination to create a whole new world. A great toy for children and adults alike.　　　¥31000

 2-31-3 Nishi Ikebukuro Toshima-Ku Tokyo ☎03-3981-1038

KISHIMOJIN TEMPLE

Kishimojin temple is very old. The temple's god encourages good growth in children. The owl figure brings good luck. This temple also features Tokyo's oldest snack stand which was established in 1781. ¥1000 each

3-15-20 Zoushigaya Toshima-Ku Tokyo ☎03-3982-8347 www.kishimojin.jp

GIGOR

Located in Shimokitazawa, a cultural town in Tokyo, Gigor makes really detailed pieces. Although they have many types of accessories, these pens is one of the most unique. Both cool and useful, they are comfortable to hold with an ideal weight to write with.These pens will inspire your imagination.

Left to Right ¥84240/¥66960/¥41040/¥50760/¥102600

 3-20-6 Kitazawa Setagaya-Ku Tokyo ☎03-3485-8382 www.gigor.jp

TOKYO 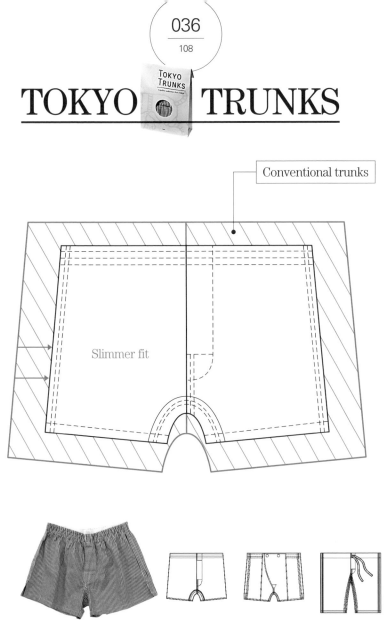 TRUNKS

Conventional trunks

Slimmer fit

These trunks were designed with comfort in mind. Many trunks are bulky and bunch up in the wrong places, but the unique and smart design of these slim Japanese trunks makes them look and feel great.

Starting at ¥3000

1-1-11 Taishido Setagaya-Ku Tokyo ☎03-3487-4883
www.tokyotrunks.com (additional location in Marunouchi)

GOTOKUJI TEMPLE

The lucky cat is a famous figure and symbol in Japan. This temple is full of lucky cat items that will bring you good luck. A cat with a raised right paw brings prosperity and good fortune, while a raised left paw attracts people and customers. Starting at ¥300

2-24-7 Goutokuji Setagaya-Ku Tokyo ☎03-3426-1437

KAMEYA

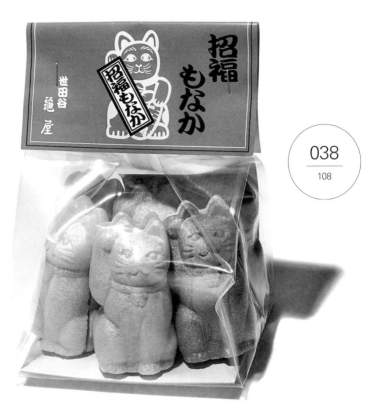

This cute package includes three different colored lucky cat monaka or waffle snacks. Filled with three types of red beans, these snacks make a lovely gift and are considered to be lucky. Some people think they are too cute to eat, but you should go ahead and enjoy their yummy flavor.

Shoufuku-monaka ¥540

3-12-2 Miyasaka Setagaya-Ku Tokyo ☎03-3429-0208

SEIJO ISHII

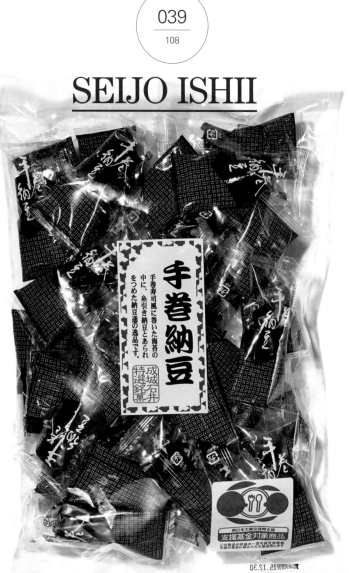

手巻納豆

手巻寿司風に巻いた海苔の中に、糸引き納豆とあられをつめた納豆通の逸品です。

成城石井
特選銘菓

Have you tried natto yet? You have to try it! But even if you don't like it you should give these snacks a try. Easy to carry as a souvenir, these natto snacks have a dry texture and a real natto taste. They are made by the supermarket SEIJO ISHII. Although there are many branches around Japan, the supermarket was established in Seijo, the Japanese version of Beverly Hills. ¥1718 (180g)

6-11-4 Seijyo Setagaya-Ku TOKYO ☎03-3482-0111
www.seijoishii.co.jp (65 branches in Tokyo)

WA SALT

つるすべ美人
お酒塩
秋田産
ぼすそると
和

温め上手
柚子塩
徳島産
ぼすそると
和

汗だしすっきり
生姜
鹿児島産

癒しさしみじみ
熊野塩

These products are made by Ishizawa Laboratories. This company's headquarters are in Omotesando, where they make a lot of toiletries and bath products. This salt is not for eating, it is a bath salt that includes special handpicked ingredients from around Japan. While in Tokyo you should enjoy a bath instead of a shower; it is the Japanese custom to make you more relaxed ¥260 each

www.ishizawa-lab.co.jp
Available at most drug stores and supermarkets.

TSUTAYA ELECTRICS

Jazz soundtracks

Musiken i mitt liv

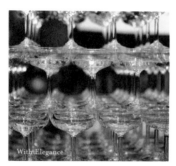

With Elegance

BLUE RIVER JAZZ

Musiken i mitt liv/Various Artists ¥2000
01.Too Good To Me/Lars jansson Trio
02.Love Is A Many Splendored Thing/Anders Persson Trio
03.A Song For You/Søren Bebe Trio
04.Latour/Lars Jansson Trio
05.Flowering Children/Lars Jansson Tommy Kotter
06.Wintersong / Lars Jansson Tommy Kotter
07.Many Season,Many Scenes,Many Sorrows/Hitomi
Nishiyama Trio
08.Folksong NO.3/Tommy Kotter Trio
09.Silently /Time Lapthorn
10.The Organist/Lars Jansson Trio

041
108

With Elegance ¥2000
01.FRANCESCO LOMAGISTRO AND BERARDI JAZZ
CONNECTION /Traffic Moods
02.MIRIAM KLEIN /By Myself
03.VERONICA MORTENSEN/Lucky
04.BRIGITTE MITCHELL/Nica's Dream
05.THE OLDIANS/One way Ticket
06.FLORIAN WEBER/Clocks
07.SHAI MAESTORO TRIO /Maya's Song
08.JOYCE COOLING /It's You
09.MARC GARY/For Hermeto
10.GIDEON VAN GELDER/Visions
11.FINN SILVER /Roadtrip
12.ALEX TAIT(THE SPANDETTES)/Event Horizon
13.ROMAN ANDRÉN/Lovin' You

BLUE RIVER JAZZ ¥1998
01.ALL OR NOTHING AT ALL / FREDDIE HUBBARD
02.THE SIDEWINDER/LEE MORGAN
03.AS/GENE HARRIS
04.A DAY IN THE LIFE/GRANT GREEN
05.CHANGE (MAKES YOU WANT TO HUSTLE)/
DONALD BYRD
06.A NIGHT IN TUNISIA /ART BLAKEY & THE JAZZ
MESSENGERS
07.FEEL LIKE MAKIN' LOVE / MARLENASHAW
08.OBLIGHTTO / BROTHER JACK McDUFF
09.NEVER MY LOVE /GRANT GREEN
10.LAMENTO/DUKE PEARSON
11.LIVING INSIDE YOUR LOVE/EARL KLUGH

Tsutaya is the most famous book shop in Japan. The Futako-Tamagawa
location has expanded their store to include high-tech electronics. The shop
has a calm, modern and artistic feel where you can buy anything from books
to a robot. A great place to spend the entire day, it also has a CD shop with
the store's original Jazz selection CDs available for sale.

VERMICULAR

Made in Japan from exceptional materials and highly advanced technology, these enamel cast-iron pots feature two double handles making them easy to carry. Accessories like organic cotton pot holders are availableas a customizable feature. Another accessory is a detachable wooden trivet that features embedded magnets. It is easy to use and protects surfaces from heat. The green "Leaf" color is exclusive to the Futako-Tamagawa location.

¥31320(22cm)/¥24840(18cm)※accessaries extra.

Organic Cotton
Heat Keeper

Organic Cotton
Pot Holder

Double
Handles

Wooden Magnetic
Trivet

eN ROUTE

eN ROUTE is one of Japan's newest boutiques and it designs a lot of fashionable clothing. It also encourages an active lifestyle, specializing in running and jogging products. This shoe case is useful for separating your shoes and keeping your bag clean. It is great for exercise and travel. ¥3564

1F FUTAKO TAMAGAWA RISE S.C. terrace market,1-14-1 Tamagawa Setagaya-Ku Tokyo ☎03-5797-3184 www.enroute.tokyo Ginza

KOSEI'S CERAMICS

Kosei Tsuji is a famous Japanese ceramic artist. His atelier and kiln are located in Tokyo. Known for his striking red pieces, he is a prodigy who has been making ceramic artwork for over 70 years. All of his pieces are handmade and therefore unique. If you would like one of his creations you should take the time to look through them and find the best one for you.

043
108

Kosei's atelier is not open to the public. However, you may be able to visit by special request. Please contact info@tsuji-ceramics.com

JIHEI MURASE

Jihei Murase is a third generation traditional lacquerware artist. He makes his pieces out of wood and paints them with a Japanese lacquer. His style is a little bit rough and all of his pieces are slim, lightweight and unique. Most Japanese lacquerware artists focus on only one part lacquerware making, but Jihei Murase does the entire process by himself. His pieces reflect his emotions and each one is made freehand.

5-27-3 Kamiuma Setagaya-Ku Tokyo ☎03-3421-6887 jihei.com

This art form mirrors classic Japanese design, when wood tableware was dominant throughout the country. This sake holder is now used as a vase.

¥486000

KAMON KOGEI

In the past, Japanese people used to adorn their homes with traditional decorations. Recently however, many of these have gone out of style as Tokyo has evolved into an exceptionally modern city. Kamon Kogei uses a traditional style and modernizes it to fit our contemporary lives. This type of decoration typically displays real rice cakes, but they are difficult to keep fresh. These ones are made of white cedar. They are simple and elegant. White cedar is often used to welcome the new year because of its clean and tidy feel. Making the rice cake shape is a difficult process and the artist uses traditional techniques to create a lifelike modern piece.

5-27-3 Kamiuma Setagaya-Ku Tokyo ☎03-3421-6887 kamon.info

This type of straw hanging ornament used to be a popular decoration. This modern version is more sophisticated. If you hang it in your entranceway it will give your home a cool welcoming feel.

Rice cakes ¥16200　Hanging decoration ¥12960

TOP HYGIA

This super-concentrated, liquid laundry detergent cleans your clothes and uniquely enhances the antibacterial properties of your laundry during washing.The more you use it, the more antibacterial properties your laundry will retain. The brand name was inspired by the Greek goddess of health and sanitation "Hygieia".   around ¥360

Available at most drug stores and supermarkets.

KANDA SHRINE

Japan is renowned for animation. Akihababra is the mecca for this subculture. You can see people in costumes and you can buy many anime items, as well as the latest electronics. Kanda shrine is the closest shrine to Akihabara. It carries a couple of special animation lucky charms. Here, amine and religious cultures fuse to create these unique items.

wooden plate ¥1500　**charm** ¥800

　　2-16-2 Soto Kanda Chiyoda-ku Tokyo ☎03-3254-0753

HILLTOP HOTEL

This quaint hotel has a very classical atmosphere where you can experience classic Japanese style. Around the hotel, there are many publishing companies. Since the hotel was established, great novelists and writers have spent time writing in the hotel's rooms. Some of the Hilltop Hotel's amenities are classical. You can get a Japanese wine carrier or a miniature version room key that will remind you of the Hilltop Hotel even when you return home.

key charm ¥1458 wine carrier ¥3024

1-1 Kandasurugadai Chiyoda-Ku Tokyo ☎03-3293-2311 www.yamanoue-hotel.co.jp

LISSAGE MEN

You should check these numbers. I has a more watery texture, II is thicker. Which one do you prefer?

These simple products were designed specifically for men's skin. The facial soap and all-in-one skin maintenizers were designed by the acclaimed creative director, Kashiwa Sato. The concept and design, including the stylish silver trigger, were created by him.

Facial soap ¥2160 Skin maintenizers ¥3640 each

//lissage.jp/men

HIE SHRINE

A large shine in downtown Tokyo, Hie Shrine's god is represented by a monkey. This leather business lucky charm is very fashionable. The mirror has a lovely design and reflects bad luck making it a popular holy item.

mirror ¥2000 lucky charm ¥1000

HATOBUS

You can find this famous yellow sightseeing bus in Tokyo. The Hatobus company has many options for sightseeing tours in the city. If you have time, you can get a ticket for the yellow bus and see many interesting seasonal events. This cute coin case is modelled after the popular bus. A lucky coincidence, the color yellow close to money brings good fortune. ¥600

 1-10-15 Marunouchi Chiyoda-Ku Tokyo ☎03-3201-2725 www.hatobus.co.jp

MUJI to Go

MUJI is famous brand that was founded in Japan and has become known worldwide. In front of Tokyo station, Kitte Department store carries a limited product that features a map of Tokyo on a foldable, reusable bag. This bag is made from the same fabric that paraglider's canopies are made from. Keep this in your bag when you go shopping and you will always carry a memory of Tokyo with you. ¥1500

3F 2-7-2 Marunouchi Chiyoda-Ku Tokyo ☎03-5220-3120

HAMACHO TAKATORA

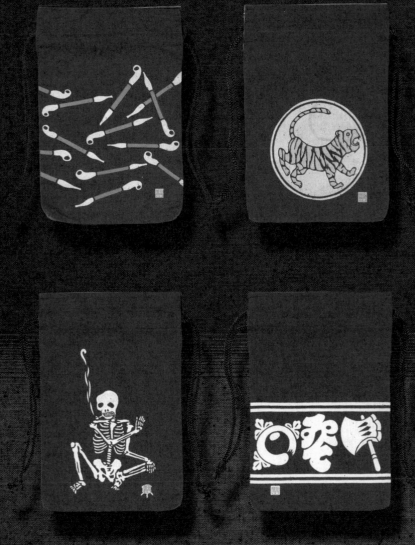

Hamacho Yakabra is a specialized dye shop that carries many traditional hand dyed pieces. These small bags are a useful way to store your items. There are over 200 different variations. This material is called Bonito stripes. People in Japan's Edo period really loved this type of fabric. Japanese words and symbols are dyed on the front of the bag. You can customize the back by adding your name.The inner lining also varies, so make sure you choose your favorite.

Bag ¥3888 each Bag with customized name ¥3780/may take up to a few days to process

OONOYA SOHONTEN

座蜂商標
やの本

御見本が御座居ますから
御遠慮なくおためし下さい。

特別に細足袋
細の普通足袋
やゝ甲高足袋
特別甲高足袋
普通新富形足袋
新富町大野屋徳本店

メートル法に依る足袋文数表

メートル	該当文数
28.0cm	12文
27.0cm	11文半
26.0cm	11文
25.5cm	10文7分
25.0cm	10文半
24.5cm	10文3分
24.0cm	10文
23.5cm	9文8分
23.0cm	9文7分
22.5cm	9文半
22.0cm	9文3分
21.5cm	9文
21.0cm	8文7分

新富町大野屋總本店

Many Kabuki actors order these socks. They are called tabi and are an old, traditional style of sock. You can get a miniature version made with the same techniques and materials as the originals. Sometimes rare fabrics or patterns are available. These black and gold decorative tabi are super rare. If you can find them, you are lucky! ¥1080

2-2-1 Shintomi Chuo-Ku Tokyo ☎03-3551-0896 www.oonoyasohonten.jp

054

108

mont-bell

mont-bell

mont-bell is a Japanese outdoor brand which uses high techniques and high quality materials. This lightweight down inner jacket is compact enough to fit in your bag, but provides a lot of warmth. It is thin enough that it can be hidden discretely underneath your regular jacket. You can also wear it on its own for a cool urban look. ¥11664

MONTBELL TOKYO KYOBASHI 3-1-1 Kyobashi Chuo-Ku Tokyo
☎03-6214-1861 www.montbell.jp (13 branches in Tokyo)

KIYA

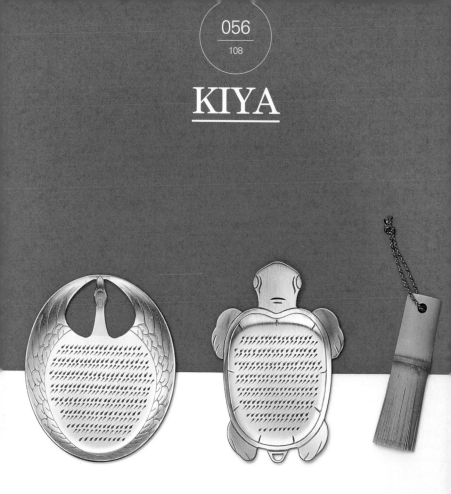

Since 1792, Kiya has specialized in knives, but they also make these charming crane and turtle spice graters. Cranes and turtles are symbolic in Japan, and when seen together, they represent a super long life. Don't forget to buy the matching brush, it makes removing spices from the graters really easy.

Crane ¥2268　Turtle ¥2268　Brush ¥648

 COREDO Muromachi 1F 2-2-1 Muromachi Nihonbashi Chuo-Ku Tokyo ☎03-3241-0110
www.kiya-hamono.co.jp (additional location in Futako-tamagawa)

SHIROKIYA DENBE

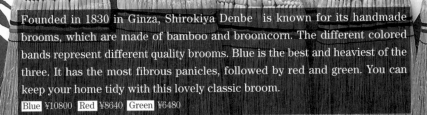

Founded in 1830 in Ginza, Shirokiya Denbe　is known for its handmade brooms, which are made of bamboo and broomcorn. The different colored bands represent different quality brooms. Blue is the best and heaviest of the three. It has the most fibrous panicles, followed by red and green. You can keep your home tidy with this lovely classic broom.

Blue ¥10800　Red ¥8640　Green ¥6480

3-9-8 Kyobashi Chuo-Ku Tokyo ☎03-3563-1771 www.edohouki.com

HIGASHIYA

Established in 2003, this confectionery shop is always moving forward. Humanity is always progressing and this shop's philosophy is the same. Higashiya not only makes confectioneries, but tableware too. This afternoon tea style is typical in the UK, but Higashiya created a Japanese version. You can use this set to showcase food, or as a unique way to store your accessories. The frame is collapsible and is easy to store.

Afternoon tea stand | Frame ¥19440 | Plate ¥9180×2 | Set ¥37800

This is a transportable tea and sake warmer. Using water and a candle you can heat up your drink. The copper material changes color as time passes making it more beautiful each day.

"Shukanki" tabletop drink warmer ¥41040

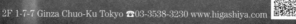

2F 1-7-7 Ginza Chuo-Ku Tokyo ☎03-3538-3230 www.higashiya.com

KOHRYU

Miyamoto Shoko carries a great quantity of sterling silver items. This ravishing teapot is made by the talented silversmith KOHRYU. Made of silver, this teapot is handmade and looks stunning. The final design features over 1000 studs. It looks traditional and modern at the same time. A silver teapot keeps your water hotter for longer, and looks beautiful. ¥118800(13.5cm)

MIYAMOTO SHOKO
1-9-7 Ginza Chuo-ku Tokyo ☎03-3538-3511 www.miyamoto-shoko.com

WAKO

Wako is a common meeting place in Ginza. This landmark has a giant clock tower on its peak. The building houses a specialty store that carries many elegant items. Their signature handkerchiefs have a stunningly rich style and feature subtle prints of the building. ¥2160

4-5-11 Ginza Chuo-Ku Tokyo ☎03-3562-2111
www.wako.co.jp (additional location at Haneda Airport)

GINZA FUGETSUDO

Ginza Fugetsudo is a specialty Japanese sweets shop in Tokyo. If you buy some sweets here you have the option of adding this bamboo gift box for a small fee. It looks nice and can be used to store things after. Although it is not expensive, the weave is very beautiful and decorative.

Available in two variation, ¥350 each

6-6-1 Ginza Chuo-Ku Tokyo ☎03-3571-5000

HASUI KAWASE

Dimensions	23cm × 21cm ¥16200
With frame	45cm × 37.5cm ¥23760

This print is also available in card form. It was chosen by Unicef as their donation Christmas card. ¥180

Kawase Hasui is a famous wood block printing artist that has created over 600 different designs. A marvellous one is of Santa Clause in a Japanese garden. It looks like it could be a present-day scene but it was designed in 1950. You can add this to your Christmas decorations to create a beautiful festive atmosphere.

Watanabe mokuhan bijutsu gaho
8-6-19 Ginza Cuo-ku Tokyo☎03-3571-4684 www.hangasw.com

KOJU

Japan has a deep relationship with fragrance. In the past, Japanese generals really loved different aromas. Koju is a traditional Japanese aroma brand and they make a great room fragrance. This fragrance does not need power or fire. You simply open the tin and enjoy. If the smell gets too weak just scrape off the top layer of wax and enjoy the fresh aroma. This item looks and smells like Japan. It is available in three variations. Sandalwood is the most popular.　¥4320

063
108

Ginza core 4F 5-8-20 Ginza Chuo-Ku Tokyo ☎03-3574-6135(4 branches in Tokyo)

EUGLENA

Euglena is a single-celled microalgae that can be used as a source of food, or fuel, in cosmetics and so on. It contains all of the essential nutrients for humans. B.C.A.D. is a skincare brand that used *Euglena's* properties to give you beautiful skin. This is true Japanese quality and is available in a cleansing balm, a foaming face wash, a skin treatment essence, a serum and a cream. Your skin will be moist and radiant. B.C.A.D Starting at ¥3300

 1F Nihonbashi Mitsukoshi Honten 1-4-1 Muromachi Nihonbashi Chuo-Ku Tokyo
www.euglena.jp

agnès b.

Famous world-wide, this French brand recently opened a new shop in Ginza. The shop's "3 Rue du Jour" name and sheep logo are the same as those of the first shop in Paris, France. This simple pouch will add a sophisticated atmosphere to your style. Back ¥10800 Front ¥9720

agnès b. Rue du Jou Matsuya Ginza Marronnier-dori Bldg.
3-7-1 Ginza Chuo-Ku Tokyo ☎03-3535-8660

ITO-YA

The erasable ballpoint pen by PILOT has recently become a common standard in Japan. Itoya is a wonderful stationery shop and they custom-ordered a special design from Frixion. These erasable pens are incredibly useful and come in 24 colors. They are a definite must try item. ¥140 each (0.7cm)

2-7-15 Ginza Chuo-Ku Tokyo ☎03-3561-8311www.ito-ya.co.jp (8 branches in Tokyo)

UBUKEYA

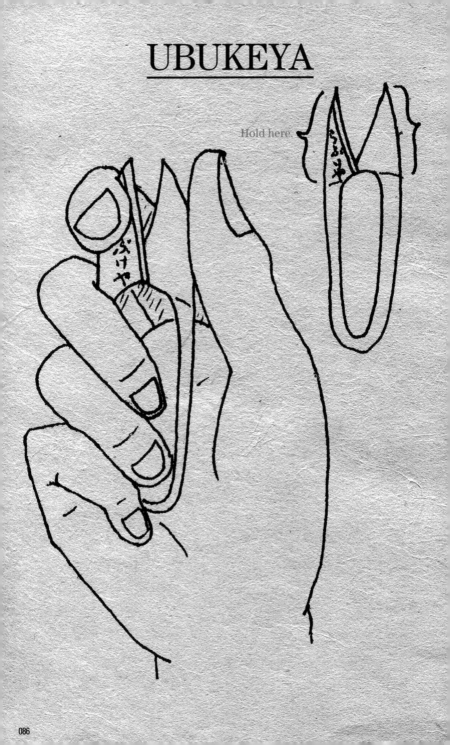

Hold here.

Established in 1783, this shop has a long history of handmade products and is famous for its knives and swords. Ubuke means baby hair. This company's scissors are so sharp that they can even trim the fine hair on your face. The father-son duo are the company's 8th and 9th generation owners. Everyday they sharpen swords and scissors. You should give these Japanese scissors a try. Their shape is modelled after the original scissor shape. Today, only Japan uses this style. It is especially useful if you work with clothing or like to sew.

¥6804

These tweezers are specially made to be 3mm thick. Japanese craftsmanship makes them stable and they feel great in your hand. This thickness is difficult to construct but its superior quality has made it a famous product of the shop.

¥11880

EDO-YA

Established in 1718, Edo-ya carries a large variety of handmade brushes. This shop's atmosphere is really cool. There are so many brushes hanging on the walls. The ostrich feather dusters are really special. Not only are they useful, but they are very beautiful too. The colored bands represent the density of feathers. Red has the highest density and green has a normal density. Green ¥9180 Red ¥12480

Magonote, the Japanese name for a back scratcher means "grandson's hand". Most Japanese magonote are made of cheap wood. Edo-ya's back scratchers are made of white cedar and are available in two versions. The soft version's bristles are made of horse hair and the hard version's are made of pig hair. With these magonote, you will never have an itchy back again.

¥1944 each

2-16 Odenmacho nihonbashi Chuo-Ku Tokyo ☎03-3664-5671 www.nihonbashi-edoya.co.jp

Optical Lens Cloth
ミクロ繊維のレンズ拭き

OZUWASHI

Optical Lens Cloth
ミクロ繊維のレンズ拭き
メガネのお手入れ
等に最適です

小津和紙

Ozuwashi is a specialty shop that carries thousands of types of paper. You can try your hand at making paper too. Also available is a special tissue used to clean your lenses. If you wear glasses or sunglasses you should give this product a try. It is made by professional paper makers and leaves your eyewear sparkling. Regular ¥540 Travel size ¥216

These standing posters are available in Ozuwashi. In traditional Japanese culture, families celebrate Girl's Day on March 3rd, and Boy's Day on May 5th. On Girl's day homes are decorated with dolls. On Boy's Day they are decorated with samurai armor. These posters are an easy way you can celebrate in your home too. ¥2700 each

IBASEN

Ibasen has been around since 1590. These sensu, or fans, are famous icons of Japanese culture and come in many different designs. Try this bamboo type fan available in 14 different colors. If you preorder, you can have a hand drawn flower added to your fan. ¥3240 each

1F 4-1 Kobunacho Nihonbashi Chuo-Ku Tokyo www.ibasen.co.jp

TSUKIJI FISH MARKET

Tokyo has a huge fish market in the bay area called Tsukiji. You can enter the market in the early morning, from 5:00 to 12:00, and visit many sushi shops as well as feel the local atmosphere. You might even see a fish auction! The fish market workers use this basket to carry fish and other things. You can buy the same one in a small shop hidden within the market.

Back ¥9180   Front ¥12480

 YAMAZAKI SEISAKUJYO 6-8-8 Tukiji Chuo-Ku Tokyo ☎03-3541-8734

MARUZEN

Maruzen is a huge bookstore. Since it was established in 1870 it has expanded to include imported items as well. This umbrella is one of Maruzen's most popular items. It is made by a famous Japanese umbrella company. Maruzen custom ordered a special slim handle design and a trademark arching canopy. This canopy produces a distinct sound when hit by falling raindrops. Owning this umbrella will make you look forward to the next rainy day. ¥16200

2-3-10 Nihombashi Chuo-Ku Tokyo ☎03-6214-2001

SHIN-YOSHIWARA

Shin Yoshiawra is a brand that is receiving a lot of recognition lately. It carries products inspired by the area's famous red light district which was prevalent from the 17th to 19th centuries. The company collaborates with traditional brands to create classic goods with a modern and often sensual twist. It gives you a taste of new Japan. Hand fan ¥1620

www.shin-yoshiwara.com (4 branches in Tokyo)

MORIGIN

Morigin is a shop that specializes in silver. This charm is a replica of a bone found in a fish called a sea bream. Japanese people call this "sea bream in sea bream" since the bone itself looks like the fish. Older generation Japanese people believed that this bone brought good luck, similar to a wishbone. Next time you eat a sea bream, which is often served as a fish head on a platter, keep an eye out for this lucky bone. Small ¥5184 Large ¥9504

074
108

1-29-6 Asakusa-Taito-Ku Tokyo ☎03-3844-8821 www.asakusamorigin.com

HANAYASHIKI

Hanayashiki, is the oldest amusement park in Tokyo. It features a roller coaster which is scary due solely to its old age. Mechanical pandas are a typical feature in old amusement parks. Put in a coin and it slowly moves while you ride it. This miniature figure doubles as an ash tray or a cute box to hold your belongings. Panda car ¥1800

2-28-1 Asakusa Taito-Ku Tokyo ☎03-3842-8780 www.hanayashiki.net

GANSO-SHOKUHIN SAMPLEYA TOKYO

Kappa bashi is an area that has many professional shops that cater to the hospitality industry. In Japan it is common to see amazing resin replicas of the food that is available in restaurants. These unique bookmarks are so realistic, they look like actual pieces of meat. Starting at ¥648

3-7-6 Nishi-Asakusa Taito-Ku Tokyo www.ganso-sample.com/en/
(Additional location in TOKYO SKYTREE TOWN)

IN REI RAI SAN

陰翳礼讃

谷崎潤一郎

中公文庫

If you can read Japanese, this book by Junichiro Tanizaki is recommended for you. Published a long time ago, this book is all about Japanese beauty. The secret, it turns out, lies in the relationship between light and shadows. If you cannot read Japanese, no problem! This book is still a cool item to own.

Available at most Book stores.   ¥514

TSUBUSHIO

This toothpaste includes a special natural salt which helps destroy bad-breath causing bacteria. It also help prevents bleeding gums and gingivitis. This product is a long selling item that has been available for over 30 years.

¥335

Available at most drug stores and supermarkets.

TOKYO NATIONAL MUSEUM

Japan's oldest and largest art museum displays a myriad of stunning art pieces. The Tokyo National Museum's gift shop carries a post card collection that is equally huge. If you are interested in Japanese art, or post cards, this is a great place to visit.   starting at ¥90

 13-9 ueno Park Taito-ku Tokyo ☎03-5777-8600 www.tnm.jp

NATIONAL MUSEUM OF NATURE AND SCIENCE

The most famous dog in Japan is Hachi. When his owner died, Hachi spent the rest of his life waiting for him to return. Japanese people, and people from all over the world love this story. Everybody knows Hachi is the famous bronze statue in front of Shibuya station, but the real Hachi's stuffed body can be found in the exhibit of the museum. Plush Hachi toys are also available for sale in the museum shop. ¥3000

7-20 Ueno Park Taito-Ku Tokyo ☎03-5777-8600 www.kahaku.go.jp

UENO TOSHOGU

This lucky charm is modelled after a traditional container used to carry medicine. The pill box is demarcated by the Tokugawa clan crest. Inside there is a tiny gold frog symbolizing a safe return journey home.

This is a cool poster of Lord Ieyasu Tokugawa's teachings. It features an old style Japanese atmosphere and cool calligraphy. This poster will give your space a wonderful feel. ¥500 each

9-88 Ueno kouen Taito-ku Ueno ☎03-3822-3455

東照神君徳川家康公御直筆寫

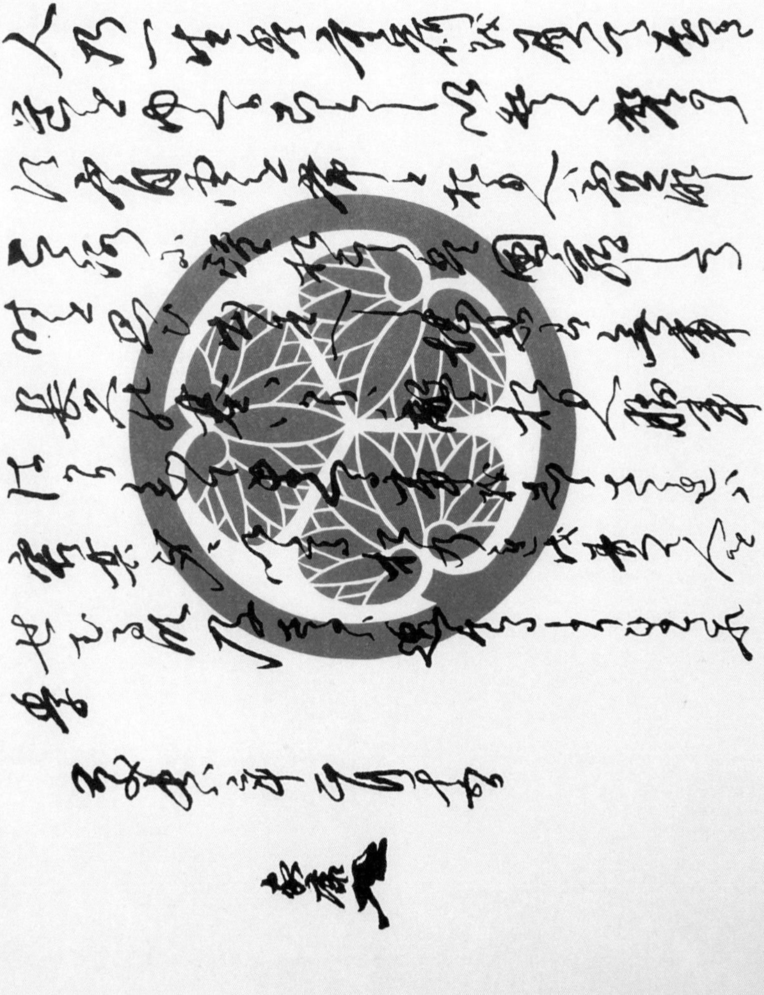
人の一生は重荷を負て遠き道をゆくがごとし
いそぐべからず
不自由を常とおもへば不足なし
こころに望おこらば困窮したる時を思ひ出すべし
堪忍は無事長久の基
いかりは敵とおもへ
勝事ばかり知りてまくる事をしらざれば害其身にいたる
おのれを責て人をせむるな
及ばざるは過たるよりまされり
慶長八年正月十五日
家康

國寶　上野東照宮所藏

EBIYA

In 1966 when The Beatles came to Japan they disembarked their plane wearing customized hanten from this unique shop. Typically worn as a type of uniform by different districts during Japanese festivals, these traditional hanten are handmade. If you have time (and money) you can customize a special order. Sometimes, the shop also has a selection of beautiful Tenugui (handkerchiefs) available for sale. prices vary

 4-6-3 Negishi Taito-ku Tokyo ☎03-3873-1587

KINTAROU AME HONTEN

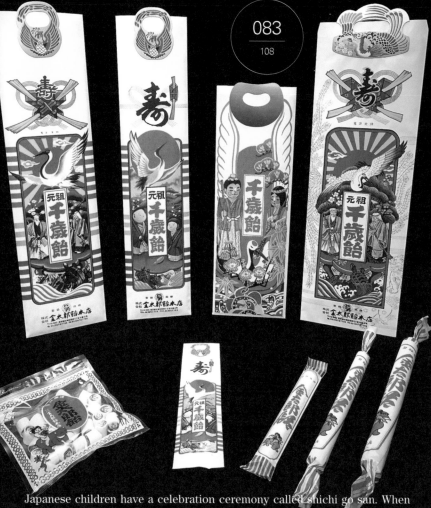

083

108

Japanese children have a celebration ceremony called shichi go san. When they are 3, 5 and 7 years old they go to shrines to pray for good health and positive growth. This celebration is symbolized by special candy. Kintarou is a famous character in Japanese tales. He is a super strong boy and is featured on the candy. The flavor is very simple and plain. This snack can be enjoyed by children and adults alike, so why not give it a try! starting at ¥170

5-16-12 Negishi Taito-ku Tokyo ☎03-3872-7706 www.kintarou.co.jp

PREGNANCY TAG

おなかに赤ちゃんがいます

If you are pregnant you should get this cute maternity tag. Available at train stations, this tag lets other passengers know you are pregnant. Passengers will be more careful around you and often offer you their seat, especially in the designated priority seating areas.

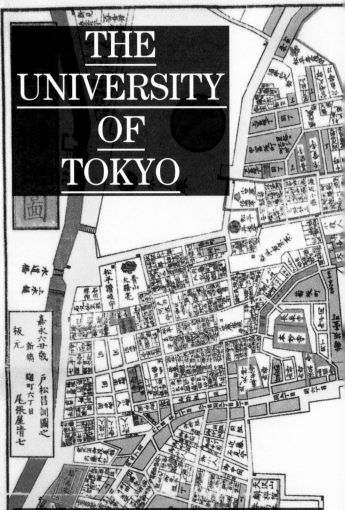

THE UNIVERSITY OF TOKYO

THE UNIVERSITY OF TOKYO is the most famous university in Japan. It has a very old history and houses many old documents. This map is a print made from an archival document in the university. It is printed on a furoshiki, which in the past was used to wrap and protect people's belongings when they went to public baths. Over time the material has been improved to become super water-repellant making it a great accessory to take to the beach, gym or a hot spring. You can also use it to decorate your home.

¥3500

7-3-1 Hongo Bunkyo-Ku Tokyo ☎03-5841-1039 www.u-tokyo.ac.jp/

TOKYO-DOME

Katori senko is a spiral shaped incense. It is a mosquito repellant commonly used in the summer months. Inspired by one of Tokyo's baseball teams, this Giants incense holder is particularly emblematic of modern day Tokyo. ¥2160

BALL PARK STORE
1-3-61 Kouraku-Bunkyo-Ku Tokyo ☎03-5800-9999 www.tokyo-dome.co.jp

YUSHIMA SHRINE

Entrance exams are a big deal in Japan. Students come and pray to the study god at Yushima shrine to get into the school of their choice. If you have an important test or exam coming up you should give ¥500 to the shrine, and the shrine's master will bestow you with this headband. It is said to bring you the god's power and help you concentrate while studying. The headband is made from the same material as the undergarments worn under a kimono. Once it is tied, it maintains its shape and does not slide off your head.

3-30-1 Yushima Bunkyo-Ku Tokyo ☎03-3836-0753 www.yushimatenjin.or.jp

UNOKICHI TACHIBANA

Unokichi is a famous calligraphy artist. He has written a lot of Kabuki play signs during his life. You can custom make an original signboard, key charm or sticker. The signboard is great because it uses Japanese lacquer which is shiny and breathtakingly beautiful. The wooden board gets darker over time, aging with you and representing your history. You can use your name or Unokichi can create a special logo for you or your company. It is an enduring piece of art. Prices vary. may take up to a few months to process. shipping available.

 UNOS 2-33-9 Yushima Bunkyo-Ku Tokyo ☎03-6240-1711 www.unos.co.jp

TOKYO SKYTREE®

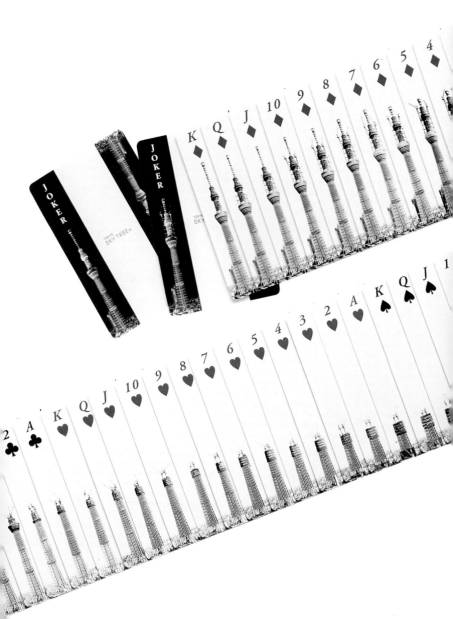

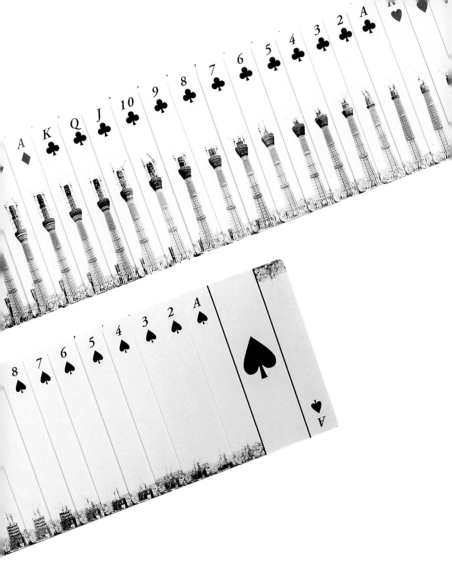

A new landmark in the city, TOKYO SKYTREE® is 634 meters tall. It is the tallest tower in Japan. In the Edo period the area surrounding the tower used to be called Musashi which means 6-3-4. This inspired the tower's final height. The tower is connected to a shopping mall where you can find many souvenirs. This card deck features progressive photographs of the tower's original construction. It is really neat. ¥441

1-1-2 Oshiage-Sumida Tokyo ☎0570-55-0634 www.tokyo-skytree.jp/

POSTAL MUSEUM

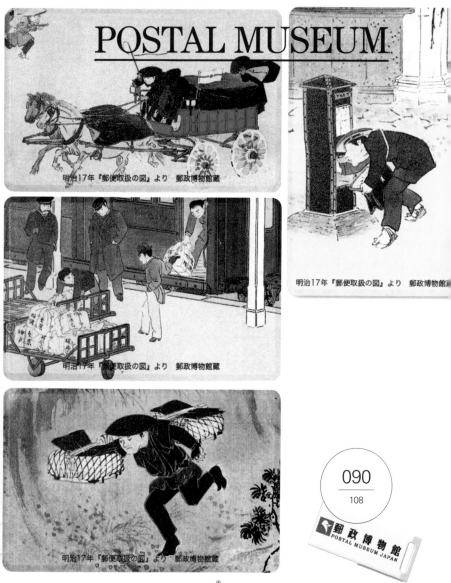

明治17年『郵便取扱の図』より　郵政博物館蔵

明治17年『郵便取扱の図』より　郵政博物館

明治17年『郵便取扱の図』より　郵政博物館蔵

明治17年『郵便取扱の図』より　郵政博物館蔵

090
108

郵政博物館
POSTAL MUSEUM JAPAN

Located inside TOKYO SKYTREE® TOWN, this museum takes you on a historical journey of Japan's postal system. The museum has the largest stamp collection in Japan featuring over 330.000 stamps. You can buy a special credit card sized picture which houses an 8 GB USB key. It is easy and convenient to carry.

 Tokyo Sky tree Town Soramachi 9F 1-1-2 Oshiage Sumida-Ku Tokyo
☎03-6240-4311www.postalmuseum.jp

¥1650 each

The Tokyo metro is the most complicated system in the world. It looks like a computer chip. If you can recognize the different stations it becomes a super convenient way to travel around the city. This card case is fashionable and available in 5 color options. You can use it to store your train pass while traveling around the city.   ¥1800 each

Metoro no Kanzume / Inside OSHIAGE Station www.metocan.com/

HIROTA GLASS

Hirota Garasu is a specialty glass company that carries many lovely pieces. This lucky cat jar is very difficult to create, and only a few people are able to make the unique shape. As a result, inventory may be low. The clear design lets you change the feeling of the piece by allowing you to fill it with the color of your choice, or you can leave it empty for a subtle touch of style.

2-6-5 Kinshicho Sumida-Ku Tokyo ☎03-3623-4145 www.hirota-glass.co.jp   ¥10800

EDO KIRIKO

Stemming from techniques in the Edo period, this shop spotlights cut glass. Edokiriko is a special technique used to create beautiful glass pieces. Typically this style is very intricate, but these glasses are simple. An odd numbered shape is said to be superior in reflecting light, and its own reflection, that's why these glasses were specifically designed with 11 sides. Resembling a European design but made with a Japanese classic technique this combination is really interesting and elegant.   S ¥12960 M ¥ 16200 L ¥ 19440

2-10-9 Taihei Sumida-Ku Tokyo ☎03-3623-4148 www.edokiriko.net

RYOGOKU KOKUGIKAN

Sumo tournaments occur three times a year in Tokyo; in January, May and September. If you have the chance you should watch a match. Did you know Sumo wrestlers use a particular hair oil made from plants to make their hair really glossy? This traditional hair oil makes your hair look beautiful. Sometimes available at Kokugikan, it can also be found in nearby pharmacies. Next time you see a bout you should look at the wrestler's beautiful hair. around ¥1100

1-3-28 Yokozuna Sumida-Ku Tokyo
Sumo bout schedule available at: www.sumo.or.jp

SEVEN GOD CLAY BELLS

095
___
108

深川七福神

恵比須神 弁財天
福禄寿
大黒天 毘沙門天
布袋尊
寿老神

There are seven famous gods in Japan. At the beginning of the year, you can take the 7 shrine and temple walking tour in the Fukagawa area to collect these clay bells. If you can collect all of the gods you will enjoy super good luck. Don't miss out! ¥300 each

OKEEI

This handmade water bucket is really difficult to make. It can be used for many purposes, such as a wine cooler or a flower pot. The bucket is made from 300-350 year old white cedar. With time the wood changes to a darker color, giving it an antique feel. The silver accents are also handmade by the company and add a stylish touch to the smooth wood. ¥54000 (limited-edition)

1-13-9 Ohghibashi koutou-Ku Tokyo ☎03-5683-7838 www.okeei.jp

EDO FURIN

Most Japanese people use furin in the summertime. They hang them beside their windows because the sound is said to help keep our bodies cool. Furin are made from many different materials. Edo or Tokyo Furin are only made of glass, and red furin in particular are believed to protect the listener's home from evil. You should choose a red furin to hang beside your window and enjoy its beautiful summer sound. **Left** ¥2700 **Right** ¥1836

SHINOHARA FURIN HONPO 4-22-5 Minami Shinozaki-machi Edogawa-ku Tokyo
☎03-3670-2512 www.edofurin.com

TAISHAKUTEN TEMPLE

Torasan, the main character of a famous Japanese TV drama was born in the Katsushika district of Tokyo. Taishakuten is the biggest temple in the area. The lucky charm that Torasan always wore around his neck is available at this temple. It features a cool and stylish check pattern.　¥1000

7-10-3 Shibamata Katsushika-Ku Tokyo ☎03-3657-2886　www.taishakuten.or.jp

HAZIKIZARU

On the way to the Taishakuten temple you can find an old shop that carries a special toy. The toy's hallmark is a cute little jumping monkey. The monkey is the servant of the Taishakuten god. When you push down on the bamboo tab, the monkey jumps up and down. Its jumping is said to ward away evil.

¥900

登録商標

OOEDO ONSEN
MONOGATARI

In the Tokyo Bay Area there is an interesting conceptual hot spring. Upon entering the building you choose a yukata and travel back in time to the Edo period. The atmosphere of the hot springs relaxes you, and if you get hungry there are many historically themed restaurants and shops available inside. Merchants in the Edo period used to wear this type of apron. You might find this apron useful for your job or hobby too. Give it a try.   ¥3140

大江戸温泉物語

2-6-3 Aomi Kouto-Ku Tokyo ☎03-5500-1126 www.ooedoonsen.jp/daiba/index.html

FUJI TV

FUJI TELEVISION

One of the most popular broadcasting stations in Japan is Fuji TV. Their headquarters building is very unique. Its focal point is a spherical shaped observatory in the middle of the building. You can go inside and gaze out at the wonderful view of the Tokyo Bay Area. You can also buy a replica case of the observatory, filled with chocolate cookies. It is very futuristic and tasty.

Spherical tin ¥864

2-4-8 Daiba Minato-Ku Tokyo ☎03-5531-1111 www.fujitv.co.jp

UMEHACHI

Umeboshi or pluns are a famous Japanese food. Have you tried them already? There are plenty of variations to satisfy everyone's tastes, including sweet, sour, salty, dried and pickled varieties. Umehachi is a special brand of umeboshi. This type is super salty, but surprisingly addictive. Try it on its own or add it to your tea or wine to experience a new taste sensation.

¥540 (60g)

3-8 Honcho Hachiouji-Shi Tokyo ☎042-627-0188 www.umehachi.com
(3 branches in Tokyo)

Mt. TAKAO

Mt. Takao is a 599 meter tall mountain. You can enjoy Tokyo's beautiful nature and lovely view of the city from the easy to reach summit.. This mountain's god is a tengu, a legendary creature found in Japanese folklore. If you have time you should explore the natural part of Tokyo.

「神通鏡」の
レンズ
だけが、
その光に
感じるん
だな。

©Fujiko-Pro,Shogakukan

FUJIKO F FUJIO
MUSEUM

KITERETSU NOTEBOOK

This notebook is from 『Kiteretsu Encyclopedia』 by Fujiko F. Fujio. The main
character used a notebook which was filled with the inventions of one of his
ancestors.This notebook has a nice, traditional Japanese look and is a fun
place to write your notes. ¥670

NOBITA'S TEDDY

This teddy bear is a key item from 『 Doraemon: A Grandmother's Recollections. As a child』, the main character Nobita, really loved this teddy bear.The red stitch marks on the bear's tummy were made by Nobita's late grandmother. After accidentally finding the bear, Nobita realizes how much he misses the days he used to spend with his grandmother. Luckily, one of Doraemon's secret gadgets is a time machine. He uses it to help Nobita travel back in time and enjoy one last day with his beloved grandmother. This story is really touching, but regardless of the plot, this teddy bear is still cute on its own. ¥4860

HYATT REGENCY
HAKONE RESORT & SPA

HYATT REGENCY HAKONE RESORT AND SPA

HYATT REGENCY HAKONE RESORT AND SPA

Tanzen

Yukata

Conveniently located about an hour from Tokyo, Hakone is a place famous for its hot springs. The Hyatt Regency in Hakone is a great place to stay. It offers the city's traditional atmosphere mixed with the hotel's contemporary feel. After a bath in a hot spring you can dress in a yukata, a traditional Japanese lounging robe. This yukata is really comfortable and its design is very unique, it is a modern take on a classic. The getta or sandals are also particular. They steer away from the typical square design and take on the modern form of a super car. **Sandals** ¥12744 **Yukata** ¥7560 **Tanzen** ¥18360

1320 Gora Hakone-Machi Ashigarashimo-gun Kanagawa
☎0460-82-2000 hakone.regency.hyatt.com

Seven-Eleven

7-Eleven convenience stores can be found all over Tokyo. Open 24 hours a day they offer a wide variety of food and beverages. In Japan, 7-Eleven also carries its own brand of stationary, with a sleek and simple design that does not distract your creativity. **Pen** ¥540 each **Notebook** ¥905 each

Stocks vary depending on the store. www.sej.co.jp (2369branches in Tokyo)

KANEROKU PREMIUM

Recommended by a famous Japanese doctor as a super supplement for your intestines, this supplement contains 7,500,000,000,000 lactic acid bacterium in one pouch! It is considered good for your health and cleanses your intestines. Adding one pouch to your drink before sleep will help keep your body healthy.

107
108

¥43200(One box includes 35 pouches)
KANEROKU Pharmaceutical ☎03-3725-4040 www.kane6.jp/product/bermkain

MAMPEI HOTEL

Neighboring Tokyo, the Mampei hotel is located in a mountainous resort area. Considered one of the best hotels in Japan, the Mampei features traditional architecture. Some rooms even have claw-foot tubs and intricately carved wooden furniture called karuizawa-bori made by Icchodo. You can buy the same furniture at a store on Karuizawa's main street.

ICCHODOU

Icchiodo is composed of a small group of carpenters. This shop was created around the time foreign Christian priests introduced Karuizawa as a summer retreat. The priests ordered special furniture which often had grape motifs. This style became a blend of Japanese and foreign tastes when the artists began to include Japanese traditional cherry blossom motifs . The product line features many pieces, including smaller items like trays. As the products age they become shinier and more beautiful.

775 Kyu-Karuizawa Kitasakugun Karuizawamachi Naganoken ☎0267-42-2557 www.icchodou.com/

925 Kyu-Karuizawa Kitasakugun Karuizawamachi Naganoken
☎0267-42-1234 www.mampei.co.jp

Map of TOKYO

Each part of Tokyo will show you a completely different face of the city. It is a wonderful place where the past, present and future merge. The items and places in this book are arranged by location. The distribution of places is not uniform, because the recommendations are genuine.

TOKYO

102

HACHIOJI

103

KAWASAKI 1

SAITAMA

ITABASHI

KITA

ADACHI

NERIMA

KATSUSHIKA

ARAKAWA
79
~
81

34

33   32

TOYOSHIMA

87   82   83
~
88   74   89
~   ~
BUNKYO   85   76   91

NAKANO   27

86   PAITO   SUMIDA

4   48   47

SHINJUKU   92
~
93

21   53   94

3   5   CHIYODA   97
~   51   54
7   23   ~   ~   EDOGAWA
52   72

SUGINAMI

18   50   96
12   8   ~
~   11   20   25   95
15   16
30

SHIBUYA   29   KOTO

35   22   24

43   17   26

38   37   44   CHUO
~
45   36   27

SETAGAYA

31   MINATO

49

MEGURO   27
&
101

41
~   100
42   SHINAGAWA

OTA

KANAGAWA

108 KARUIZAWA

105 HAKONE

TOKYO

141

This book has 108 shopping recommendations. The number 108 has a special meaning in Japanese Buddhism. It represents the 108 bonno, or earthly desires that humans have. These desires can often lead to suffering, and it is important to try to control them. Shopping can often stimulate certain bonno. This book will act like a bible for shopping. Rather than spend money frivolously on useless items, you should take the time to look through this book. You can choose something that will help you remember your experience in Japan, or you can get a gift that will make someone special in your life, happy.

Coming Spring 2016
MUST-BUYS KYOTO

Instagram: must_buys
E-mail: mustbuys3@gmx.com

PUBLISHER
Kesaharu Imai

MUST-BUYS crew
Naoki Kokubo (edit / text / photography / sales / selection)
Iga Miziała (translation / text)
Ryota Toriigahara (selection / photography)
Sherry Yamaguchi (selection)
Ichiro Ikeda (Illustration / map)
gami (photography)
Tatsuhiko Shimada (photography)
Masashi Larry Ohiwa (cover design)

PRODUCTION DIRECTOR
Shunsuke Ogawa

CIRCULATION MANAGER
Hiroshi Sasagawa

DESIGN&DTP
Lina Sugimoto (WPP)

PRINTING
Dai Nippon Printing Co.,ltd

Correspondents,
Washington,D.C.Bureau
(Pictorial Press International)
Norman T. Hatch
Mikako Burks

Publishing by WORLD PHOTO PRESS 3-39-2 Nakano Nakano-ku,Tokyo 164-8551 JAPAN
Phone +81(Japan)-3 -5385-8111 Fax +81(Japan)-3 -5385-5614

ワールド・ムック1100(通巻1100号)/平成28年1月25日発行/マスト・バイズ トウキョウ
発行人:今井今朝春/発行所:株式会社ワールドフォトプレス/〒164-8551 東京都中野区中野3-39-2
TEL:編集部03(5385)8111/広告営業部03(5385)5658/販売部03(5385)5701/印刷所:大日本印刷株式会社

©ワールドフォトプレス2016/造本には十分注意しておりますが万一、落丁・乱丁などの不良品がございましたら弊社販売部あてにお送りください。
送料弊社負担にてお取替えいたします。本掲載記事の無断転載、複製、転写を禁じます。文中の価格は消費税込みの総額表示です。